WORDS

YOU MUST SAY
TO YOURSELF TO

SUCCEED
IN LIFE

Library of Congress Control Number: 2015954447

ISBN: 978-1-63308-177-2 Paperback
         978-1-63308-178-9 Digital

Interior and Cover Design by R'tor John D. Maghuyop

CHALFANT ECKERT
PUBLISHING

1028 S Bishop Avenue, Dept. 178
Rolla, MO 65401

Printed in United States of America

WORDS
YOU MUST SAY
TO YOURSELF TO
SUCCEED
IN LIFE

300 Powerful Quotes to Self

OLUWAYEMISI M. OBE

CHALFANT ECKERT

PUBLISHING

To my dad Kayode
who always finds the simplest ways to say
the right things every time.

INTRODUCTION

I find solace and strength from these words, they have served me well. And when going through tough times, notebooks and pen became companions, and words loyal friends.

They are soothing and sometimes saving; I hope you find the same comfort and strength these words have offered me.

I really do hope they will be as loyal to you as they have been to me as we share these few moments together.

–Yemisi

1.

Don't be a person of words, rather be a person of results.
That is much better.

2.

The thing that needs conquering—
the only giant—is my attitude.

3.

I still believe the most powerful things in
the world are words; they make or mar,
build or destroy … and they are totally
submissive to the one using them.

4.

Like the sun, the wind, and water (to
mention a few), the resources and wealth
at my disposal are limitless.

5.

Everything around us is improving, technology ensures that.
The lesson there? There is always a better
way to get things done.

6.

If I have as much dedication as the sun to show
up 100 percent daily, I will produce the same effect
that creates the day and every ripple that comes with it.

7.

Dear Mind, I need your help and support
to change from the inside out. Thank you.

8.

Everything important can be learned with
commitment and hard, hard work.

9.

Criticism and attack are two separate
things ... listen for the real message.
If it is *positive*, pick it up and use it.
If it is *negative*, drop it and move on.

10.

I can sit and mope, or I can pick myself up, get to work, sweat
as hard as I can, and then pat myself for a job well done.

11.

Time will pass ... so shall I.

12.

What exactly do I want to be remembered for?

13.

If we don't learn from history, then we shouldn't be
angry when history is hard on us.

14.

If my skin can't break, so can't my heart.
I am that strong. My skin may rip, cut, or scar, but it heals. It
always heals, and so will my heart.

15.
I can…
I should…
I will, *Period.*

16.
Never judge a man. Do not even raise an eyebrow
until you have walked in his shoes under the same circumstances.

17.
What I don't know I must learn and then apply.

18.
Schooling and *education* are two different words:
misunderstood and misinterpreted.
School promotes rote learning. Education promotes
self-enlightenment. No wonder enlightened men
without schooling still can succeed, but never vice versa.

19.
Think it. Write it down. Figure a way to carry it out. Then do it.

20.
The best companions a man can have are a supportive
spouse and a book. Books, books, books. Loyalty to books
introduces a man to other things—fame, friends, and kings.

21.
If a seed can produce the whole works—stem,
branches, leaves, and abundance of fruits—over and over again
throughout a tree's lifetime, that serves as a
small indication of I am capable of.

22.

The seed gives its all. The soil gives its all.
Water gives its all. The sun gives its all.
Every element that aids growth gives its all, knowing it will be
well taken care of, and new life will be reproduced. Same goes
for creative ideas. They show up when man gives his all.

23.

Prosperity must have a more meaningful value
than money or what money can get.

24.

Riches and wealth are not twins—distant cousins, maybe.

25.

Two eyes, two ears, two nostril holes, and one mouth.
Some things are meant to be used more than others.

26.

Eyes take in. Ears takes in. Mouth takes in and gives.
Nose takes in and gives. Use all things appropriately.

27.

The only person God permits me to
have dominion over is myself.

28.

On the surface and on the inside, we all want the same thing;
we only spell it out with different grammar. With everyone deal
with respect and patient.

29.

Be careful what you do to others. Like a clock, it somehow
finds its way back to the starting point.

30.

Make up the inside of yourself as much as you do the outside.
Details of the inside find a way to the surface.

31.

Life doesn't listen to our desire; it works with
the seeds we preserve inside our mind.

32.

Listen to your first gut instinct; consider the second thought
with care, because it usually travels with doubt ... pay
attention to the third and ignore it if it takes you far from the
gut feeling. The gut feeling is usually the right one—most of
the time.

33.

I once heard a man say, "Quit trying to lose weight,
because you tend to search for the things you lose. That is why
you put it back on." It made all the sense in the world.

34.

I murder ideas most of the time; I need to break that habit.

35.

I am custom-made; I must seek and find what works for me.

36.

Things I ignored remained, at least until I
made a decision about them to actually "do" it.

37.

Practicing the right principles makes the perfect life.
When you choose to do it, be prepared for
its consequences good and bad.

38.

Decide—just *decide* and work it out.

39.

Round your life up in one word;
I may have to explain it but mine is ENIGMA.

40.

Most impactful word for me ever—
Responsibility. Self-responsibility.

41.

"Work doesn't kill, laziness does," my father once told
me. First it steals from you and then leaves you for dead.

42.

Life is a choice. So is love, friendship, wealth,
poverty, and a whole list of other stuff.

43.

The way you address people says a lot
about the kind of person you are.

44.

Lessons learned, some are forgotten,
but I have more scars than lost memories.

45.

To inhale fresh breath, I first have to
exhale and release the old air.

46.

Learn the new things to replace the old ones.
Learn new good things to replace the old bad ones.

47.

Anger: When I feel the surge rising within me, I always ask
myself what am I really angry about? Is it voices from
the past or is this a matter of the present?
That makes all the difference.

48.

I am 100% what I think and say I am.

49.

If someone is doing what I want to, living how I want to, I
should ask myself what they know that I don't.

50.

Waiting is different from patience. One is
the static, and the other is not.

51.

Whether you like it or not, 'save' a portion of your money
at 20% as the minimum.

52.

It all starts in the head with a thought.
Then it becomes a monster or an ally.

53.

I am learning to live with myself peacefully and lovingly.
I have no choice; it is a "till-death-do-us-part" affair.

54.

"Do you truly need that?"
Ask three times before you bring out your wallet or card.

55.

I am stronger than I give myself credit.

56.

If you don't have self-discipline, life will
assign a taskmaster for you.
The prison is the most popular example of that.

57.

Experience should not be the best teacher;
there are better ones in people and books.

58.

I have to listen to myself more.

59.

Sometimes I am absolutely sure of myself, most times, well,
I needed to work on my confidence, a lot.

60.

Love isn't hopeless.

61.

After the hurt, brokenness, and tears ,another
chance will always show up if I am open enough.

62.

Listen to everything; sieve out the jargon.

63.

I believe in me. I will keep saying that to
myself until I actually start to act it.

64.

There is always a second chance, and a third, and then a fourth.
The only challenge is the time wasted not getting it the first time.

65.

A seed sown in time produces its reward in time.
Delayed sowing means delayed reward.
No sowing, no reward.
It is as simple as that.

66.

Let the decision be yours, so you can live with its consequences.

67.

Your thoughts are powerful. They take on a
life of their own without permission
and bring you results that are outcomes of those thoughts.
You can think good thoughts as well.

68.

I wonder why I remember the hurts more than the good times.
I am pretty sure that is a fraction of the story.

69.

I am grown, yet I am learning to communicate
and to interact properly.
I learned wrong the first time around.

70.

Any time I waited to be approached first,
I lost opportunities to make great friends.

71.

Everyone has a story to tell.

72.

Pain cannot be spoken, but it is always in the eyes,
which always say it all.

73.

Listen to what people aren't saying more
that what they are saying.

74.

I trust myself; I can take my own advice.

75.

When I open my mouth, Dear Lord, may my words
add value to the person I am talking with.

76.

Sometimes I am afraid of my own thoughts;
deep down I feel they might confront me with what
I knew all along but didn't want to face.

77.

When I need something outside of myself, I pick my Bible,
connect my knees to the floor, and that's
when things begin to happen.

78.

I can't be everything, but I can be the
best of who I was created to be.

79.

Twinkling stars of my yesterday are leading me
to the bright, shining sun of tomorrow.

80.

What is this moment—this very moment —saying to me?

81.

I have to define my greatness and one thing I
know for sure: it is nothing like anyone else's.

82.

There must be a seed of greatness in me, for it stirs when I see
another human achieve spectacular accomplishments in any field.
It doesn't matter if it's an Olympian or a singer who aces a song.
That tells me it's not the act, but the seed that produced that act.

83.

Hundreds of voices swirl in my head; a word of advice
from everyone I ever came in contact with, but I never
really found mine to be the strongest and the loudest.
Now I have to do just that.

84.

Mince your words, and let their proceeds
make you feel good about yourself.
That way you know the person it is
directed to feels the same way.

85.

I need to learn to be assertive.
I am reacting again.
The goal is to be proactive.

86.

Unlike any other time, I told myself, I have every
right to be in the room as everyone else.
Immediately, I felt good about myself. I stood
up, walked around, chatted rather than hiding in
the corner of the room and acting invisible.

87.

Oh pen and paper, you are my best friends tonight.
I know you will keep my secrets safe.

88.

If I believe enough, everything will be possible for me.

89.

I am worth it; I deserve every good thing in life.

90.

If it crosses my mind, then there must be a way to get it.

91.

When "he" walks up to me, I feel my walls go up quickly.
Now, I need to demolish those walls even faster, every time.

92.

Forgiveness is a must; my must.

93.

He said, "I believe in your future." Those were the sweetest
words I had ever heard and the most important ones to me.

94.

My father once said, "You have the tendency to be lazy,"
and I slipped into that mode for a while. One day I said
to myself there must have been something he saw, a habit
maybe. If I truly have the tendency to be lazy, then I have
the tendency to be diligent. 50/50 right? Then I understood
the message. He had such high expectations of me.

95.

I have always treated myself last, serving everyone first.
By the time it gets to me, I am all knocked out.
So I decided I would take care of me first, so I would have
much more to offer, and it worked.

96.

Be patient with people. Everyone is going through something.
Everyone has a story to tell. Everyone has
potential; and that includes me.

97.

What I know is not all there is to a matter.
Thus, it is okay to seek, in fact, it is wise as well.

98.

It is okay to say *"No"* sometimes.

99.

I am trying to remember most of the things my
parents told me, now I know I wasn't listening.
I thought I knew everything. What a shame.

100.

I have always felt success, satisfaction,
and happiness was location-bound.
So, I relocated only to discover this was
wrong. It was *me*-bound.

101.

Meet and challenge your enemy within.
Somehow you will overcome
even when you feel you don't have the strength.

102.

The greatest gift I have is me.

103.

The best thing that can happen to me is me.
Now how I treat me will determine the
results I will get out of me.

104.

All knowledge is in vain, except when applied as action.
It will all make sense, eventually, LOL.

105.

Who I am and who I was created to be is totally
dependent on me. I can decide to remain in the same
spot or recharge to become better.

106.

A man makes his own way; no one hands it over
to him. When you decide to be something and
work towards it, you can then become it.

107.

I asked myself: If I were to die today, what is the
one thing everyone who knew me would say about
me? Will what I am thinking about doing right
now be very important in those last minutes?

108.

In my life, I matter the most.

109.

When you do the right thing for the wrong
reasons, you only get complicated results.

110.

There always comes a time for elimination.
The earth rejuvenates in seasons.
Trees and flowers let go of their identities as the
old identities die, and new ones are born.
The shedding is not the end, but the beginning of a new phase.

111.

Beauty is not about having a pretty face.
It is about having a pretty mind,
a pretty heart, and a pretty soul.

112.

Always dream with your eyes wide open.

113.

Everyone has his own destiny and the right to follow it through.

114.

It always feels good to take charge,
no matter what the circumstances are.

115.

I intend to embark on the do-it-now mission.

116.

Just do it, and do it now.

117.

I intend to teach myself self-reassurance.

118.

I intend to break my fearful habit.

119.

Be thick-skinned so that you can handle anything
and everything life throws in your path.

120.

Renew your mind.
Break old thinking habits.
Retrain yourself on how to think right.

121.

As much as you can, look your best.

122.

Overall, I am smart and intelligent enough.
Overall, I have the ability to figure things out.

123.

I choose not to see any experience as a failure.
I choose only to see it as an opportunity to begin again.

124.

Do not stop looking, searching, and learning.

125.

Common try: If you don't try, you will never know.

126.

I know I CAN!

127.

I lift my eyes to the hills;
I believe, I really do believe it is well.

128.

When ego is lost, limitations are lost.
You become infinite, kind and powerful.

129.

There are simply no accidents.
Everything is ordered by a divine hand.

130.

It's only a phase.
This too shall pass.

131.

Build faith in yourself for yourself.

132.

Every day is a miracle, and so am I.

133.

I came; I showed up for that.
I am glad I did, and I am better.

134.

I can't write my story until I live it … that
is when I truly have something to tell. It is
not too late to live the dream.

135.

Most of the time, "no" means
"Not *NOW*; try again later."

136.

My mindset: A plus or a minus?

137.

I still wonder what makes successful people succeed.
Are they destined to or were there just unseen principles they
applied that set them apart?

138.

I can rewire myself to create the life I want.

139.

I can't help others until I help myself.

140.

It is my road and mine alone …
Others may walk it with me, but no one can walk it for me.

141.

Pay attention: to life and to details.

142.

I need to stop and think about what I'm spending money on.
Is that something I need?
If not, then it's really not worth it.

143.

You can take all I have; I have the capacity to do it all over again.

144.

God is all-in-all; life-proof.

145.

Deal with people as individuals. Never pass on aggression.

146.

No one owes me anything.

147.

For everything I get, I am grateful always.

148.

Expect good things to happen to you and be
willing to work for what you want.

149.

Reach out to people, even if with little gifts.
It might be their last hope and last ray of light.

150.

Be good to everyone.
You don't know who is who
… Or who they can be.
You might need help and they might be there to help.

151.

Be smart enough to know which friendships
to keep and which to walk away from.

152.

Be mindful what you put out there,
what you tell others about yourself.
Be mindful what kind of conversation you get involved in.
(What goes around always come around.)

153.

Don't be afraid to be different.
Just be a good different and choose the good habits.

154.

It is your life; think it through and make your decision.

155.

Feel other people's pain. Be human enough to see and feel them.

156.

Do not feel bad that good things are happening to you or
that people react to it. You deserve it as much as anyone.

157.

Once I realized I was no longer afraid to be alone,
I discovered I loved myself more. I choose silence or
calm music, because I enjoy my own company.

158.

Always think things through before you act.

159.

A wise man once said, *"Make a project of
your life; be strategic about it."*

160.
What I expect is what I get, eventually.

161.
If we all entered the world on equal grounds,
then I have 100% chance of success.

162.
"What will people say?" is popular, but, most of
the time, those people are too worried about the
same thing to fully concentrate on you.

163.
I have an equal chance as everyone to succeed.

164.
The choice is mine to make something and someone of myself.

165.
How I see something determines whether it is
an *opportunity* or an *obstacle*.

166.
In nine months, a newborn is formed
and then continues to grow into an adult.
I will be patient with the changes I intend
to see in myself as I work them out.

167.
With time, I will begin to believe what I hear or tell myself.
I can, as well, hear me moving towards my goals.

168.

If you are afraid to make a decision, you are more
likely to be influenced into something totally wrong for you.
I am smart enough to create things I want.
Anything else not promoting that idea is a lie.

169.

What am I saying to myself right now?

170.

If everyone in the world was to write the
names of people who most influenced them,
how many times would my name come up?

171.

If you can be of help, don't think twice.

172.

In this matter, how real are you?

173.

Would you want a child like you?
A parent like you?
A friend like you?
A staff like you?

174.

Let your life speak for you without you
even having to open your mouth.

175.

I remember the things I didn't do more
than those that I accomplished.
That tells me a lot about decision-making.

176.

If someone else is doing it, then I can,
maybe not the same way. Maybe even better.

177.

One more step forward.

178.

Are ants smarter than me? They don't even have brains.

179.

I can, I can, I can.

180.

What is the lesson here?

181.

My mirror spoke to me this morning.
I am not proud of what it said.
But it gave a word of advice: "You can be better."

182.

One question I ask myself more often lately:
Are my fears only in my head?

183.

Nothing important comes in the mail without
an order. Nothing tangible will come out of life
if you don't place an order for it, too.

184.

I have to earn respect from myself first before
anyone else can give it to me.

185.

You earn respect; demanding it is useless.

186.

Everyone faces challenges; you've got to face yours.

187.

What do you want to do right now?

188.

Someone somewhere in the world has or is facing far worse than
you can even imagine and came out or is coming out stronger.
Lesson? I have no excuse.

189.

Who does what isn't important? It is what I do that is.

190.

If I have to tell a story, any story at all,
would I be proud to tell mine?

191.

What is the lesson in the story? And the story in each lesson?

192.

I am strong, I am strong, I am so strong.

193.

There is no one rule that fits in two lives.
Everybody's got a peculiar path to walk.

194.

I will write my achievements in pen and mistakes in pencil.
That way I can use my eraser more.

195.

Everything and everyone has the territory where
they strive. Only on mine will I strive.

196.

I dare me to be my best—my very best.

197.

I can rebuild into the life of my choice.

198.

The person I need to conquer is the person
behind the eyes I see when I look into the mirror.

199.

Life makes no promise of withdrawal:
I get nothing except what I expect and work towards.

200.

Everyone you want to be has already been taken by the one who bears the name or has the life. You have to be 100% yourself everyday until the payday, and everyday after that.

201.

Don't let fear drive you, let love fuel you.

202.

I am at ease with money, just as I am with the air I breathe.

203.

I am learning … daily.

204.

I have mastered the act of being invisible.
Now I am learning to stay effectively visible.

205.

In every failed attempt, I asked myself:
"What is the lesson to learn?"

206.

I am still failing, **but** I am also learning.

207.

I don't allow anyone to tell me my fears are not real. Acceptance of that fact empowers me to confront them.

208.

In details, what lifestyle will I be comfortable with and how do I make it happen?

209.

What you say to yourself, within yourself, truly matters.

210.

Look inward or outward;
Whichever way you look, ensure that you are
learning, thinking, and discovering.

211.

What were the most important words anyone
ever said to you? Why were they important to you?
Start from there.

212.

If your thoughts were projected, would
you be having the same thoughts?

213.

To prosper or to survive requires just about the same energy.

214.

Eventually all that will really matter is who you became
in the process and whose lives you impacted.

215.

I have come to accept that although there may be
some kind of luck at play, successful people work
really hard for the luck to become a success.

216.

The most important things in life can't be bought;
better attention should be given to them.

217.

If you are hurt by the past, you may be broken,
but don't stay down … and don't stay broken.

218.

The sun always shows up every morning.
That is the height of assurance.
Trust that much that things will get better.

219.

There is always one thing going well for you.
Search for it, even if you have to search really hard.

220.

Three things—say hi, give a smile, and give a wave—
to three total strangers today.

221.

Always believe in the start of something new.

222.

Pain is in my past; my future is filled with possibilities.

223.

Somehow I always make it through,
and somehow things always get better.

224.

I can do all things through God who gives me strength!

225.

So, what is the game plan for the next phase?

226.

Plan, but move to execute.

227.

Everything around me is teaching something.

228.

Every invention and upgrade reminds me
there is always room for improvement.

229.

If I believe it hard enough, I will figure ways to work it out.

230.

If I don't try, I won't find out of what I am truly capable.

231.

There's always a way out; even if it's only a crack.

232.

Opportunity is like pregnancy.
You never know exactly what you will receive.

233.

I have the capacity to create and modify my life.

234.

Experiences are paths already walked;
there are lessons hanging on its sleeves.

235.

Everything is perspective-based. There is always a different view.
Because I have never done it before doesn't mean I can't do it.

236.

A new lifestyle and a different kind of
achievement requires a different kind of mindset.
Always, always re-educate yourself.

237.

Expose your mind to the world that can be.

238.

Inward or outward—
The change has got to be at both ends.

239.

I can be good. I can be great.
I can be greater than great.

240.

Fear should motivate you, not stop you in your tracks.

241.

If I have to write my memoir,
what will I say … what will I be most proud of?

242.

I can change; I just need to believe it
hard enough and get back to work.

243.

Feelings you cannot trust … but your gut, absolutely.

244.

Because I don't have it yet doesn't mean it doesn't exist
… that includes wealth, that includes fame.

245.

Yes, you can quit.
But only the bad habits and everything
that belittles you.

246.

Quit the excuse and do something about that something.

247.

Once you walk in …
& stay in …
You will see results.

248.

Sweat it out. See it melt, whether it's the weight or the challenges.

249.

I am strong enough.

250.

Today, I become my greatest fan.

251.

Each day is mine, I own it.
I will shine so bright, it will be hard to ignore me.

252.

Everything I need I already have.

253.

Nothing changes when nothing is done.

254.

Was I crazy enough today?

255.

Success is in doing.
Real success is in continuous doing.

256.

My need will not meet me on my knees
with my head in my hands.
It will find me working hard, prepared and ready for its visit.

257.

The normal me = My comfort zone
Now I look at the *it*, do the opposite, and try to commit to it.
The new me = My conquering zone.

258.

If things are working around me, but not for me the way
I want, then the one who needs a checkup will be me.

259.

Fame is not unattainable; it only takes huge commitment.

260.

If you cry or sweat, it doesn't matter.
Only make sure they are for the right reasons.

261.

Whatever you want to be, that's fine, but ensure
anyone who crosses your path always will have a
pleasant memory of their encounter with you.

262.

Competition is limiting because it has
an invisible yardstick already.
But the stretch of "creating" is endless.
It has nothing to measure up to, only the
expectations of the one who owns it.

263.

May I not know how to take myself too serious
and miss the best of fun that life has to offer.

264.

Like a bamboo tree, I already have in me all I need to succeed.
Now I have to nurture the inside and reproduce.

265.

I believed in limits, and it became my reality, but it was a lie.
Now I have to develop muscle and a new
mindset to build a new life.

266.

I could ride with fear, but I chose not to anymore.

267.

No one wakes up great.
Everyone great woke up and worked hard into it.

268.

A little twinkle star is more notable by many than a
beam of light shining from the ground.
Do not become popular on common ground.
Aim higher; aim for excellence.

269.

Ants can easily be crushed, but no bird can fly by unseen.

270.

I am not inferior or superior to anyone. Neither is anyone to me.

271.

Love may be risky,
but loneliness is the worst kind of risky.

272.

Think in long- and short-term.
Do not make a long-term decision using short-term thinking;
it works the other way around, too.

273.

Permit your mind to function as it has been created to be.
It is that powerful, powerful enough to carry you through a
lifetime and still have more to offer. You cannot use it up.

274.

Any decision you make has two fan bases—one is cheering
and one is booing. Ensure, in the end, it serves you well,
serves others well, and is solidly good enough to
drown out the booing side.

275.

If your life is to become a biography,
will you be proud about the story told of you?

276.

It is okay to be stupid, as long as you are learning
something and not occupying that seat for long.

277.

Life is all about the interpretation you
give to what comes your way.

278.

A wall could be a dead end or a barrier to be scaled.

279.

For every product that gets to me, there are hundreds
of businesses and money made, whether manufacturing,
packaging, logistics, transporting, marketing,
or sales. Opportunities around me are endless.

280.

In every good relationship, there are two imperfect people
committed to paying the price for staying together
and making the most of that agreement.

281.
Notebooks look more attractive when written in.
The handwriting, the drawings, the pen
color, and the cancellations.
A blank notebook, on the other hand,
is just that, blank and boring.
So is the life of someone who has made mistakes more attractive
than the life of someone was has been too careful to try.

282.
I only remember the names of those who made an impact on
my life, and I only remember the opportunities that I did not
take.

283.
It is good to be patient, but sometimes you need to get on your
feet and hit the road to make your patience worthwhile.

284.
Always be generous with the potential in people.
Deal with them based on it, because no one can
predict the future. You will never know if the person
will come to be the lifeline you will need.

285.
Everyone has a motive, be pure in yours.
With it, you will walk through life on safe grounds.

286.
Be good to all; and all will be good to you too,
even when you don't know how that is going to be.

287.

You cannot be dry. The deeper you drill yourself,
the deeper your core you will discover.

288.

Smile as much as you can to as many as you can.
It might be a gesture that will save a life, and you will be
rich in the amount of smiles you will get in return.

289.

When you can help, do it to your capacity not
because you want something back, but because
if you were in those shoes, you would want
someone to do the same for you.

290.

My fears simply melt once I actually face them.
Then I wonder what took me so long.

291.

Be careful what you say to everyone and how you
say it. You do not want to be that person that breaks
the final cord of hope someone is holding onto.

292.

Life is like a loan borrowed from a bank. We all will pay
back with detailed account of how we spent or invested it.

293.

If you run, you will keep running.
If you stay and face your fears, you just might win big.

294.

Like a pregnant woman, you alone can
bring the dream you carry to live.

295.

If you do not know yourself,
you will not live to your full potential.
Then the chance given to you was wasted.

296.

I am bold enough to create a path for myself.
It doesn't have to be one someone else already made.

297.

Learn to say sorry.
Learn to say thank you.
Know when to use either.
Know when to use both.

298.

Most of the time I am the solution I need,
I can always find a way to resolve a matter.

299.

Do not just make every moment count; that is ineffective.
Make it count for you, for those in your
life, and those that cross your path.

300.

I cannot lose my essence.
I will not bow to worry, pain, or fear.
I chose to keep my head up.

Last Notes:

Autumn sheds the leaves and Spring brings them back. Winter
gives so much cold, while Summer gives so much heat.
I have so many lessons to learn from the four seasons of life.
When am at a loss and cannot hear myself speak, I find
someone to inspire me. I find a song to move me into action
to spring me out of my jaded moment.

Life experiences are like sliding a strand of thread through
the eye of a needle. You get to the other side before what you
went through becomes useful to you or those around you.

Priorities make life not necessarily easier, but smoother.
When all things are in place, then you can allocate
the right amount of you in the accurate fashion.

***Put a piece of you into all that you do … And then pass it on.*

Twitter: Oyemmyc

Instagram: oyemmyc

Tumbler: oyemmyc

Facebook Page: Yemisi Obe

Google+: Yemisi Obe

Website: www.yemisiobe.com

email: oluwayemisiobe@gmail.com

Note from the Publisher

Are you a first time author?

Not sure how to proceed to get your book published?
Want to keep all your rights and all your royalties?
Want it to look as good as a Top 10 publisher?
Need help with editing, layout, cover design?
Want it out there selling in 90 days or less?

Visit our website for some exciting new options!

www.chalfant-eckert-publishing.com